An Emerald (

EXPLAINING ASTHMA

LIVING WITH ASTHMA

An Emerald Guide to

EXPLAINING ASTHMA

LIVING WITH ASTHMA

Ellen Baxendale

Editor: Roger Sproston

Emerald Guides
www.straightforwardbooks.co.uk

Emerald Guides

ISBN 978-1-80236-170-4

Printed by 4edge Ltd www.4edge.co.uk.

Cover design by BW Studio Derby

Whilst every effort has been made to ensure that the information contained within this book is correct at the time of going to press, the author and publisher can take no responsibility for the errors or omissions contained within.

CONTENTS

*

*

Introduction

Asthma deaths rise by 30% in a decade

Deaths from asthma are at their highest level for a decade, with a third more people dying last year than in 2008. Experts believe that as many as two thirds of the 1,422 fatalities recorded last year could have been prevented with better basic care but said most of the 5.4 million people in Britain living with asthma were still not receiving the recommended treatment and advice.

Samantha Walker, director of research and policy at Asthma UK, said it was especially concerning that there had been a steady year-on-year increase. "We need to be taking a really intelligent look at this," she said. "If we keep on seeing this increase, that's really worrying. This is a trend for a significant increase in asthma deaths that we can't explain. One possible factor could be pollution, with a higher death rate recorded in southeast England. The data, for England and Wales, showed that child fatalities remained rare, with under-14s accounting for between ten and 20 of those who died of asthma each year. However, the number of adult fatalities has increased consistently. The largest rise, of 42 per cent, was seen among 35 to 44 –year-olds. Dr Walker said that while the charity did not know what was behind the trend, it was clear that people were still not taking the condition seriously. She stated:

"Doctors, nurses and people with asthma are complacent. This means that the basics are being overlooked." Simple interventions such as a written plan of action for how to respond to an attack and being taught how to use an inhaler properly can dramatically improve survival. Kay Boycott, chief executive of Asthma UK, added that the statistics showed that thousands of people had died needlessly in the past ten years. "The same mistakes are being made again and again because essential recommendations have not been implemented. This lack of action is costing lives and devastating families and communities."

Covid 19 and Asthma

Although lockdowns, due to the pandemic, are now in the past (and hopefully stay there) Covid 19 is still about, along with the aftermath, Long Covid. There is a lot of advice on various websites concerning asthma and Covid, in particular asthma.org.uk. Below I describe briefly the main concerns relating to asthma and Covid but for more fuller details you should visit the aforementioned website.

Coronavirus generally

If you have any of the main symptoms of coronavirus you should stay at home for at least five full days and avoid contact with others until you feel well and no longer have a high temperature.

Is it coronavirus or an asthma attack?

COVID-19 can cause symptoms, like breathlessness and coughing, similar to asthma. But a high temperature, tiredness, and changes in taste or smell do not usually happen with an asthma attack. These symptoms are more likely to be due to coronavirus infection.

If you've tested positive for COVID-19 or have coronavirus symptoms you may be wondering how it's going to affect your asthma and what you should do now.

Five key things you need to do:
1. Stay at home and avoid contact with other people
2. Manage your coronavirus symptoms
3. Keep taking your usual asthma medicines
4. Follow your asthma action plan
5. Act quickly if your asthma symptoms get worse

Coronavirus and asthma – what's the risk?

Studies suggest that the majority of people with asthma may be at *slightly* higher risk of serious illness from coronavirus than the general population.

But the current guidance is based on evidence that shows the risk for people with asthma is *significantly* less than other conditions, which means that most people with asthma are not at higher risk from coronavirus. If you've had both your COVID-19 vaccines, your risk of serious illness from coronavirus, and being hospitalised, is likely to be low. Booster jabs top up your protection and lower your risk from new variants, so it's important to get your booster jabs too.

Will coronavirus make your asthma worse?

You could feel worse with coronavirus because you already have trouble breathing. However, studies do not suggest an increased risk of an asthma attack when you have

What coronavirus treatments are there?

There are treatments available to treat coronavirus. These are available to people (aged 12 and over) who test positive for COVID-19 and are most at risk of serious illness from the virus. The NHS will confirm whether or not you're eligible to be assessed for these treatments. If you are eligible you should be sent free lateral flow tests to keep at home. This is so you can test as soon as possible after developing typical COVID symptoms. If the result is positive, the NHS will then contact you about accessing treatments. If you don't hear within 24 hours, call your GP or specialist, or 111.

Treatments are best started as soon as possible after a positive test, even if your symptoms are mild. The treatments currently available are:

- A monoclonal antibody treatment - sotrovimab (Xevudy)
- Antivirals- molnupiravir (Lagevrio), nirmatrelvir and
- ritonavir (Paxlovid) and remdesivir (Veklury).

- have had a positive lateral flow test
- feel unwell with symptoms that started in the last five days
- are aged 50 or over, or 18-49 with an underlying health condition.

Recovering from coronavirus

It can sometimes take people a while to recover from coronavirus infections, even if they have been mild. If you have extreme tiredness, breathlessness, or a cough that just doesn't seem to be settling as you would usually expect, you may have Long COVID.

Talk to your nurse, GP, or hospital specialist if you think you may have long COVID or if your coronavirus symptoms aren't going away. Your healthcare professional can assess what care you need, which may depend on whether you were treated in hospital or at home.

Long COVID and your asthma

When you're recovering from coronavirus, it is important that you're able to recognise the difference between ongoing coronavirus symptoms and any asthma symptoms flaring up. Your asthma is more likely to:
- cause a wheeze
- cause a change in your peak flow score
- improve with doses of your reliever inhaler.

It is important that you carry on treating any asthma symptoms as usual. Stick to all your usual prescribed asthma medicines.

*

It is the intention of this book, updated to 2023, to highlight all aspects of asthma generally and put forward ways to prevent asthma deteriorating further.

As we will see in chapter 1, asthma is a common lung condition that causes breathing difficulties. with varying degrees of severity. It affects people of all ages and often starts in childhood, although it can also develop for the first time in adults. There's currently no cure, but there are simple treatments that can help keep the symptoms under control, so it doesn't have a big impact on your life.

This comprehensive book, divided into seven parts, with two appendices dealing with welfare benefits and travel, looks at the causes of asthma and what can be done to alleviate them and what treatments are available. The book also looks at the things that can be done by the individual to minimise the effects of asthma.

Overall, the information contained within should be of significant help to those who suffer from asthma and its effects.

****

Part 1: What is Asthma?

Chapter 1

What is Asthma and How Widespread Is It?

We have all heard of asthma, either through the news or, more commonly, through family and friends. Asthma is a long-term condition, that is it is usually with people for life. It affects the airways, or the tubes that transport air in and out of the lungs that swell and produce mucus. For some people, asthma is seen as a minor nuisance, flaring up every now and again, which can be controlled. However, for others asthma is a serious problem and can be potentially fatal if not treated right.

A brief history

Asthma is not a new condition; in fact there are written, documented proofs of asthma patients' and their treatments from ancient Egyptian times. In the 1870s, the Georg Ebers Papyrus containing prescriptions written in hieroglyphics, and which had over seven hundred remedies for asthma, was found in Egypt. This prescription talked about an asthma medication to be prepared by mixing herbs and heating them on a brick. This was done so that the patient could inhale the fumes. Also, centuries ago the Chinese started inhaling beta-agonists obtained from herbs that contained ephedrine.

Asthma is a Greek word that is derivative of the verb aazein, which means to breathe out with open mouth or to breathe heavily. The phrase asthma made its first appearance in Homers The Iliad, which had the meaning of short-drawn inhalation. In short, asthma is a disease that has been around for thousands of years. However, as time has moved on and medical science has progressed, we now know more about asthma and its triggers and symptoms and are able to control it more effectively.

Symptoms of asthma

The most common symptoms of asthma are:
- Shortness of breath
- Chest tightness or pain

- Trouble sleeping caused by shortness of breath, coughing or wheezing
- A whistling or wheezing sound when exhaling (wheezing is a common sign of asthma in children)
- Coughing or wheezing attacks that are worsened by a respiratory virus, such as a cold or the flu

Asthma-facts and figures (2022-2023)

According to Asthma UK:

- 5.4 million people in the UK currently receive treatment for asthma (1.1 million children and 4.3 million adults)
- Every ten seconds someone is having a potentially life-threatening asthma attack in the UK
- On average 3 people die from an asthma attack in the UK every day
- Around 200,000 people in the UK have severe asthma. Severe asthma is a debilitating condition that doesn't respond to usual treatment and can cause people to be in and out of hospital.

Asthma across the UK

England

More than 5.4 million people are currently receiving treatment for asthma. This consists of 932,000 children and

3,600,000 adults. For more detailed statistics go to: www.asthma.org.uk.

Scotland

368,000 people (1 in 14) are currently receiving treatment for asthma. This includes 72,000 children and 296,000 adults.

Wales

314,000 people (1 in 10) are currently receiving treatment for asthma. This consists of 59,000 children and 256,000 adults.

Northern Ireland

182,000 people (1 in 10) are currently receiving treatment for asthma. This includes 36,000 children and 146,000 adults.

The aim of this book isn't to bombard the reader with lots of facts and figures. If more information is needed, as mentioned above, Asthma UK www.asthma.org.uk is a good site to start with. There are also other sites such as the British Lung Foundation www.blf.org.uk.

In Chapter 2, we investigate the different types of asthma that exist and the causes of particular forms of asthma.

Asthma triggers

(See overleaf)

ASTHMA TRIGGERS

Exposure to various irritants and substances that trigger allergies (allergens) can trigger signs and symptoms of asthma. Asthma triggers are different from person to person and can include:

- Airborne substances, such as pollen, dust mites, mould spores, pet dander or particles of cockroach waste
- Respiratory infections, such as the common cold
- Physical activity (exercise-induced asthma)
- Cold air
- Air pollutants and irritants, such as smoke

- Certain medications, including beta blockers, aspirin, ibuprofen (Advil, Motrin IB, others) and naproxen (Aleve)
- Strong emotions and stress
- Sulfites and preservatives added to some types of foods and beverages, including shrimp, dried fruit, processed potatoes, beer and wine
- Gastroesophageal reflux disease (GERD), a condition in which stomach acids back up into your throat

If you come into contact with one of the asthma triggers it can cause your airways to react in one of several ways:

- the muscles around the airways tighten so that the airways become narrower.
- the lining of the airways becomes inflamed and will start to swell
- a sticky mucus or phlegm sometimes builds up which can narrow the airways even more.

Read more about asthma triggers, particularly triggers within the home, such as dust mites in Chapter 3.

The risk factors associated with asthma
(See overleaf)

Asthma Risk Factors

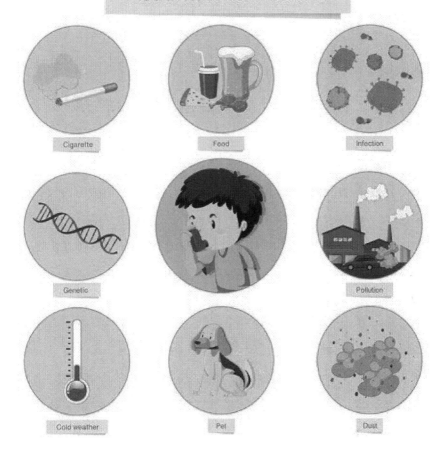

There are a number of factors which are recognised as predominant risks and which increase people's chances of getting asthma. These are:

- Genetic factors, I.e., having a blood relative who has asthma
- Being overweight
- Being a smoker

- Having prolonged exposure to second hand smoke
- Exposure to some other types of pollution such as living near a busy polluted road
- Exposure to pollution through the workplace
- Having another allergic condition that can trigger off asthma. This might be dermatitis or hay fever.

Asthma attacks

Every 10 seconds someone has a potentially life-threatening asthma attack. An asthma attack is when your asthma symptoms get significantly worse. The attack is caused by a sudden tightening of the muscles around your airways, which is known as a 'bronchospasm'.

During the attack, the lining of your airways will become inflamed and swollen and will thicken with mucus. These three factors combined make it more difficult to breathe and produce an attack. Asthma attacks are very common but, as has been pointed out, can be life-threatening. Many of the subsequent deaths, up to 3 a day according to the NHS, could be avoided with proper treatment and awareness of how to deal with an attack.

How can I tell if I am going to have an attack?

Asthma attacks tend to be the result of your usual asthma symptoms getting gradually worse over a few days and going unnoticed. If you need to use your reliever inhaler more than three times per day, this could be a sign that your symptoms are not being managed properly, putting you at risk of an attack.

Symptoms of an asthma attack

The symptoms or signs of an asthma attack include:

- shortness of breath
- wheezing
- coughing
- rapid breathing
- tightened chest and neck muscles
- children often complain of tummy or chest ache
- panic or anxiety
- suddenly pale and sweaty face
- bluish fingernails or lips
- inability to speak
- your peak flow score is lower than normal

The symptoms won't necessarily occur suddenly. In fact, they often come on slowly over a few hours or days.

Peak flow test

Peak flow is a simple measurement of how quickly you can blow air out of your lungs. It's often used to help diagnose and monitor asthma.

A peak flow test involves blowing as hard as you can into a small handheld device called a peak flow meter. These are available on prescription or can be bought from most pharmacies. By measuring how fast you're able to breathe out, your peak flow score can indicate whether your airways are narrowed.

This could be a sign that you have asthma, although other tests such as spirometry will often be needed to confirm the diagnosis.

Spirometry is a simple test used to help diagnose and monitor certain lung conditions by measuring how much air you can breathe out in one forced breath. It's carried out using a device called a spirometer, which is a small machine attached by a cable to a mouthpiece. Spirometry may be performed by a nurse or doctor at your GP surgery, or it may be carried out during a short visit to a hospital or clinic.

If you've already been diagnosed with asthma, measuring your peak flow regularly can be a useful way of monitoring your condition. Your score can show whether or not your condition is getting worse. It can also check if your medication is working and indicate whether you're having an asthma attack. Measuring your peak flow before and after exposure to a possible asthma trigger, such as something you're allergic to or a substance you're exposed to at work, may also show if anything in particular causes your symptoms.

Measuring peak flow

The first time your peak flow is measured, you'll be taught how to do it by a doctor or nurse. After this they may advise you to carry out the test regularly at home using your own peak flow meter.

To measure your peak flow:

- find a comfortable position, either sitting or standing
- reset your peak flow meter so the pointer is pushed back to the first line of the scale – this is usually 60
- hold the peak flow meter so it's horizontal and make sure that your fingers are not obstructing the measurement scale

- breathe in as deeply as you can and place your lips tightly around the mouthpiece
- breathe out as quickly and as hard as you can
- when you've finished breathing out, make a note of your reading

This should be repeated 3 times, and the highest of the 3 measurements should be recorded as your peak flow score. If you're monitoring your asthma at home, you may have a diary or chart to record your score. You can download a peak flow diary from the Asthma UK website if you don't have one.

Peak flow score

Your peak flow score – also known as your peak expiratory flow (PEF) – will be displayed on the side of your peak flow meter. This is given in litres of air breathed out per minute (l/min). What's considered a normal score depends on your age, height and gender, you should ask your GP or asthma nurse for more information on what would be considered a normal score for you.

A significant difference between your score and a normal score, or a difference in your scores in the morning and evening or when your symptoms are good and bad, may suggest you have asthma. If you're monitoring your asthma at home, your score should be compared to your best result at a point when your condition was well controlled. A big difference between your current and best score could be a sign that your condition is becoming poorly controlled or that you're having an asthma attack.

Peak flow is low

If you have a personal asthma action plan, it might say what you should do when your peak flow score falls to a certain level. You may just need to use one of your inhalers, or you may need to seek medical help.

If your reliever (blue) inhaler is not helping reduce your asthma symptoms, or is not lasting for more than four hours, then you are having an asthma attack and should follow the instructions below.

What are the signs of a severe asthma attack?

In some cases, asthma attacks can cause severe symptoms. A severe asthma attack may make you feel agitated and confused. Your chest may feel very tight and you may find it difficult to speak. If you are experiencing continued difficulty breathing and are not getting sufficient oxygen, your lips may show a blue tint.

(See diagram overleaf)

It is important that you use your reliever inhaler as soon as you feel that you are experiencing the first signs of an asthma attack to avoid severe and potentially life-threatening symptoms.

What to do when you have an asthma attack

Asthma UK gives the following guidelines for children and adults to follow when having an asthma attack:

- Try to stay calm
- Sit up straight (don't lie down or put your head between your legs)
- Take 1 puff of your reliever inhaler every 30-60 seconds, for a maximum of 10 puffs or if you have an inhaler spacer - put 10 puffs of salbutamol in to it and breath in and out slowly.

If you do not feel better after 10 puffs, call 999 for an ambulance. If you feel worse or are worried at any stage, call 999 for an ambulance. If your ambulance is taking longer than 15 minutes to arrive, repeat steps 1-3 while you wait.

What to do after an attack

After having an asthma attack, there are three things you should do:

- Book an appointment with your doctor or asthma nurse to be seen within 48 hours of being discharged from the hospital.
- Make sure you have been shown how to manage your asthma properly and use your inhalers by an asthma nurse or doctor and make a written 'action plan' for future attacks and daily management of your symptoms.
- Book a catch-up session with a specialist from the hospital to be seen in 1 month to review your treatment plan and asthma symptoms.

If you still need to use your reliever inhaler regularly after an asthma attack, the dosage of your treatment may need to be adjusted by a doctor. You should not have to use your reliever inhaler more than 3 times per week. Even if your symptoms of asthma are mild, you are still at risk of having a potentially dangerous asthma attack. This is why it is so important to take your asthma medicine as prescribed by your doctor, and to reduce your risk of an attack by following this advice:

Make sure you are on the right asthma treatment by visiting your doctor at least once a year for a check-up and to discuss treatment option. Remember to take your prescription inhaler regularly by following the instructions given to you by your doctor.

Stay healthy and take regular exercise.
Monitor your usual asthma symptoms so that you are aware if they get worse over time or get much worse very quickly.

Make an 'action plan' (see appendix 2) to follow when you have an asthma attack with the points above: Asthma UK have found that this method reduces the risk of having to go to hospital for asthma by four times.

****

Part 2: Different Types of Asthma

Chapter 2

The Different Types of Asthma

As we have seen in Chapter 1, asthma is a long-term condition, that is it is usually with people for life. It affects the airways, or the tubes that transport air in and out of the lungs which swell and produce mucus. For some people, asthma is seen as a minor nuisance, flaring up every now and again, which can be controlled. However, for others asthma is a serious problem and can be potentially fatal if not treated right.

We will now look at the different forms of asthma. Although different organisations seem to have slightly different categories, because it is difficult to provide precise definitions, I have started by using the broad categories as identified by Asthma UK which are:

- Occupational asthma
- Severe asthma
- Difficult to control asthma
- Adult-onset asthma
- Childhood asthma
- Seasonal asthma

Occupational asthma

Occupational asthma is caused by, or can be worsened by, exposure to substances over time in the workplace. They can cause asthma in one of 3 ways:

- An allergic reaction
- An irritant reaction
- Gradual reaction which results in the buildup of naturally occurring chemicals such as histamines in the lungs resulting in an asthma attack

Typical workplaces with high rates of occupational allergens include:

- Bakeries, flour-mills and kitchens where flour dust and additives in the flour are a common cause of occupational asthma.
- Hospitals and other healthcare settings can have triggers like natural rubber latex proteins found in latex gloves, as well as particles and vapours from surgical techniques.
- Pet shops, zoos, and animal laboratories expose you to allergens like pet fur, dander, and saliva, and dusts from animal enclosures.
- Farms and agricultural workplaces produce a range of agricultural dusts such as grain dust, poultry dusts.

Other dusts are produced that are a mix of materials from fungal spores, bacteria, endotoxins, mites, animal dander and faeces. Dusts are the most common cause of occupational asthma among agricultural workers.

Workplaces with high rates of occupational irritants include:

- Car manufacture and repair workshops expose workers spraying cars and other vehicles to a chemical called isocyanate (typically in 2-pack paints). Isocyanate is the most common cause of occupational asthma.
- Woodwork and carpentry workshops produce dusts from hardwood, softwood and wood composite when it is machined or sanded.
- Electronics and assembly industries expose people to irritants from fumes from rosin-based solder flux.
- Engineering and metalwork workplaces – people who work in machining or shaping are exposed to metal working fluids (MWFs) which can cause occupational asthma if you inhale the mist or vapour.
- Hairdressing salons can expose workers to chemical irritants such as hairdressers' bleach containing persulphate, and henna.
- Indoor swimming pools expose workers like lifeguards or swimming teachers to airborne chloramines. This is when the chlorine in the water reacts with bodily

proteins creating an airborne irritant in the air around the pool.

In addition, there are numerous substances used in various industries that can trigger occupational asthma including:

- Chemicals such as adhesives, shellac and lacquer, plastics, epoxy resins, carpeting, foam and rubber, insulation, dyes (textile workers), and enzymes in detergents
- Proteins in animal hair and/or dander
- Grains, green coffee beans, and papain (an extract of papaya that may trigger a latex allergy)
- Cotton, flax, and hemp dust, commonly found in the textile industry
- Metals such as platinum, chromium, nickel sulfate, and soldering fumes

Signs and Symptoms of Occupational Asthma

Symptoms of occupational asthma include general symptoms of an asthma attack, such as coughing, wheezing, chest tightness, shortness of breath, and breathing difficulty. Eye irritation, nasal congestion, and/or runny nose may also be present. As stated previously, this can be allergy-related or an irritant reaction from exposure to asthma triggers in the workplace.

If you think you have occupational asthma, ask your health care provider about a referral to an asthma specialist. The specialist will perform a detailed exam, including taking your past medical history and reviewing current breathing problems. After any necessary asthma tests, the specialist will develop an asthma treatment plan, which will include asthma medications, such as bronchodilators, asthma inhalers, and inhaled steroids to control your asthma. It will also be important to avoid any asthma triggers at work.

Preventing asthma attacks caused by Occupational Asthma

Preventing asthma symptoms by reducing exposure to the triggers at work is the most important step you can take to reduce the occurrence of occupational asthma. It's also important to use appropriate asthma medication to prevent symptoms. Even with the right asthma medications, continued exposure at work can make asthma more difficult to control. The Health and Safety Executive (HSE) www.hse.gov.uk is a government agency that has created guidelines that determine acceptable levels of exposure to substances that may cause asthma. Employers are required to follow these rules.

However, if in a particular job, exposure to asthma triggers is unavoidable, most employers are willing to assist the employee to find a more suitable workplace. Once it has been determined what causes your asthma, discuss with your health care provider how best to approach your employer and what precautions need to be taken. Reducing exposure to the triggers at work is the most important step you can take to reduce the occurrence of occupational asthma. It's also important to use appropriate asthma medication to prevent symptoms. Even with the right asthma medications, continued exposure at work can make asthma more difficult to control.

What your employer needs to do

Your employer has a duty under the Health and Safety at Work Act 1974. This means they must minimize any exposure to hazardous substances in the workplace. If your work involves you having contact with allergens or irritants, this should have been explained to you before you started work. You should also have completed a brief health screen check, including a breathing test at the start of your employment. This is something you need to do again, every year, to make sure you're not developing asthma. If you do develop occupational asthma your employer should notify The Health and Safety Executive.

How is occupational asthma confirmed?

Make an appointment to see your GP so you can talk about your job and the substances you're exposed to at work. Tell them about any symptoms you've noticed, like sneezing, runny nose, or conjunctivitis (itchy, red, inflamed eyes), or shortness of breath, cough, chest tightness or wheeze. To help confirm or rule out a diagnosis of occupational asthma, your GP will want to know if:

- your asthma symptoms started as an adult, or your childhood asthma symptoms have returned since you started working
- your symptoms improve on the days you're not at work or on holiday
- your symptoms get worse after work or disturb your sleep after work.

If your GP suspects occupational asthma they may:

- refer you to a specialist in occupational medicine
- offer blood tests or skin prick tests to confirm any allergies. (If your symptoms are triggered by irritants, rather than allergens, this won't show up in an allergy test.)
- ask you to keep a peak flow diary, so they can look at your peak flow scores both at work, and at home
- offer you a 'challenge test' if it's been difficult to find out exactly which substance at work is triggering your asthma. This is where you're asked to breathe in substances thought to be causing your symptoms to see if any trigger your asthma symptoms. It's quite a difficult test so it will only be done in specialist centres where you can be closely monitored.
- Prescribe a preventer inhaler to deal with underlying inflammation; and a reliever inhaler so you can control symptoms when they come on.

Can occupational asthma be cured?

Unlike pre-existing asthma, the symptoms of occupational asthma can go away completely if they're identified soon enough, and you stop being exposed to the trigger. For some people, their symptoms stop as soon as they're no longer in contact with the trigger; for others it can take a bit longer. Sometimes symptoms don't go away completely or can go on for years. This is usually because your occupational asthma wasn't spotted soon enough, or your symptoms were more severe.

Even if your symptoms do go away though, the substance that set them off will always be a trigger for you, so you'll need to avoid it, which means avoiding similar workplaces.

Difficult to control and severe asthma-Severe asthma

A person who is diagnosed with 'severe asthma' has a specific type of asthma that doesn't respond to, or get better, with the usual medications. About 200,000 adults and children in the UK are diagnosed with severe asthma.

The causes of severe asthma

There are a number of theories concerning the causes of severe asthma:

- **Eosinophilic asthma.** Eosinophilic asthma is a type of asthma caused by increased levels of inflammation in the airway due to white blood cells called eosinophils.

- **Inflamed airways.** Airways are inflamed to a level that medications can't reduce the inflammation enough to clear your airway.
- **Environmental triggers.** The cause of the airway inflammation is a chemical or other environmental irritant that medications cannot easily control. This is often from occupational exposure.
- **Obesity.** Obesity may cause your asthma to become severe and more difficult to treat.
- **Poor treatment adherence.** Not adhering to the treatment your doctor prescribed to manage your asthma.

Developing severe asthma

Severe asthma can develop at any age. It can change from normal levels to severe levels over time, or it can be triggered more suddenly by certain factors such as pneumonia or hormonal changes. Most people who are diagnosed with severe asthma already have an asthma diagnosis.

Risks of long-term damage to the lungs

One of the potential long-term effects of severe asthma is something called 'airway remodelling'. This is where your airways become thicker over time, so the airway itself is narrower, making it harder to breathe. This can happen as a result of frequent asthma attacks, which may happen more often. Changes to the structure of the airways can be avoided with good asthma management. There are three things that you can do:

1. Make sure that you go for regular reviews of the medicine that you are taking to check how well they are reducing your symptoms.

2. Try your best to work out which pollutants and irritants such as dust, fumes and pollen affect you so that you can avoid them as much as possible.

3. If you smoke-QUIT.

Complications of severe asthma

Long-term severe asthma can sometimes lead to a chronic lung condition called COPD (chronic obstructive pulmonary disease) or ACO (Asthma COPD overlap).

Severe asthma treatment-Medications

The definition of severe asthma is that it either doesn't respond to treatments and medications at all, or it's very difficult to treat. This lack of response to medications, known as therapy-resistant asthma, may be because your asthma has become resistant to corticosteroids or other medications used to treat asthma. Other medications and treatments that you can try for severe asthma may include:

- corticosteroid injections
- higher doses of inhaled corticosteroids

- using inhaled corticosteroids more frequently
- continuous inhaled nebulizer
- ipratropium bromide aerosols
- long-acting beta-agonists (LABAs)
- montelukast
- theophylline
- oral corticosteroids

The medications listed above may be used alone or in combination to try to get your severe asthma under control.

Lifestyle changes

The following lifestyle changes may help in the treatment of your severe asthma:

- when possible, remove or avoid any allergens or exposure to environmental irritants like chemicals
- gradually lose weight if you're obese, under the care of your doctor
- avoid known triggers whenever possible
- work with your doctor to find a treatment plan you can follow strictly
- As mentioned above, don't smoke

Difficult to control asthma

Most people with asthma achieve good symptom control with inhaled therapies but approximately 5-10% of asthma sufferers in the UK continue to experience difficult to control asthma. Such patients have an increased risk of death, experience greater morbidity, have a reduced quality of life and often have adverse side-effects from drug therapy.

There is no precise definition for difficult-to-control asthma, but it is associated with the number of symptoms patients have and how much treatment they require. Patients who continue to have uncontrolled symptoms despite standard therapy require referral to a difficult-to-control asthma clinic. The benefit of such a clinic is that a systematic evaluation can take place that may reveal factors contributing to the individual's symptoms. It can take 6-12 months to establish a diagnosis. There is no consensus about what investigations should be performed, but a detailed assessment, including lung-function testing and compliance with therapy is required.

Patterns of difficult-to-control asthma

Assessment of symptoms and exacerbation rates over a period of time can help to establish types of difficult-to-control asthma.

However, ongoing trials have identified the following types of difficult-to-control asthma and the treatment for each:

- Fatal or near-fatal asthma - usually associated with hypercapnia (high concentrations of carbon dioxide in the arterial circulation) and/or the need for mechanical ventilation despite treatment. These patients often require frequent courses of oral corticosteroids.

- Brittle asthma type I - there is consistent wide variation in symptoms and lung function tests despite regular medication at high dose.

- Brittle asthma type II - characterised by severe episodes of airway narrowing that occur rapidly over minutes or hours with no obvious trigger. Patients have a background of normal lung function and/or well-controlled asthma. They often require short periods of mechanical ventilation. This type of asthma is extremely rare; it has been suggested that it accounts for only 0.05% of people with asthma.

- Airway narrowing - patients require continuous low doses of oral corticosteroids with intermittent increases to high doses (from 40-60mg prednisolone/day). These patients are known as steroid-dependent asthmatics.

- Aspirin-induced asthma - usually associated with rhinitis, sinusitis and nasal polyps (known as Samter's Triad). These patients are sensitive to non-steroidal anti-inflammatory drugs (NSAIDs) such as aspirin. A severe asthma attack can occur within three hours of ingestion of an NSAID.

- Premenstrual asthma - this has a very distinct pattern, with symptoms occurring within two to five days of the onset of the menstrual bleed. Once the bleed has occurred the symptoms disappear and the lung function returns fully to normal. This type of asthma is usually responsive to beta-agonist therapies.
- Adult-onset asthma - patients who develop asthma after the age of 21 years often have difficult-to-control asthma. The reason for this is unknown, but despite high doses of therapy and/or continuous oral corticosteroids they usually remain symptomatic.

It can take time to understand the different types of asthma, but knowing the type experienced by a patient can assist with planning that individual's management and treatment regimen.

Is the diagnosis correct?

It is important to have a diagnosis of asthma confirmed or to identify whether there is another cause for the patient's symptoms. A structured history should include details of childhood asthma, allergies, any admissions to intensive care with respiratory problems and past and current treatment. Detailed lung-function assessment includes the following tests:

- Spirometry - to measure airflow from the lungs and lung volume.
- Gas transfer - to measure the ability of the lungs to transfer a trace amount of carbon monoxide into the pulmonary circulation.
- Airway resistance measurement - a method of determining the patency of the airways during tidal breathing.

Asthma treatment should be withheld before performing lung function investigations; for example, the use of short-acting bronchodilators should be stopped for four hours before a lung function test. Patients may find this stressful, so it is important that the nurse reassures them that they are safe and that action will be taken if they become symptomatic. Reversibility testing, which measures whether there is an increase in airflow following the inhalation of short-acting bronchodilator medication, is the most common lung-function test for diagnosing asthma, but patients may also be given a histamine challenge to identify airway hyper-responsiveness.

Factors contributing to loss of asthma control
There are a number of medical factors that may contribute to loss of asthma control.

Some of these are discussed in more detail below.

Psychological factors

Factors such as anxiety, depression, denial of having the disease and the lack of appropriate medical care have all been identified in patients with difficult-to-control asthma.

Concordance with medication

"Medication concordance" is a term used to signify that the doctor and patient have come to a shared agreement about therapeutic goals. It is merely one end point; to have reached it the doctor would have had to develop a rapport with the patient, understood the illness in his or her terms, come to a shared understanding and agreement about the condition.

A recent evaluation of a group of patients with difficult-to-control asthma found that almost 50% did not take their inhaled medicine. Although adherence to prescribed medicines is notoriously difficult to assess, prescription monitoring, weighing inhaler canisters and taking blood tests for theophylline, prednisolone and cortisol levels are all methods that can be used to obtain a more detailed picture of the extent of patients' concordance with their prescribed medicines.

Many factors can influence concordance. For example, patients misunderstanding their treatments, denying they have asthma, or their social situation. Providing patients with information about their treatments, educating them about their disease and building an open and honest relationship can assist in identifying factors that influence an individual patient's attitudes and beliefs towards their medicines. Discussions concerning concordance must take place during the initial assessment and periodically while the patient is under review.

Adult-onset asthma

When a doctor makes a diagnosis of asthma in people older than age 20, it is known as adult-onset asthma.

Among those who may be more likely to get adult-onset asthma are:

- Women who are having hormonal changes, such as those who are pregnant or who are experiencing menopause
- Women who take oestrogen following menopause for 10 years or longer
- People who have just had certain viruses or illnesses, such as a cold or flu
- People with allergies, especially to cats
- People who have GERD, a type of chronic heartburn with reflux
- People who are exposed to environmental irritants, such as tobacco smoke, mould, dust, feather beds, or perfume.

The difference between childhood asthma and adult-onset asthma

Adults tend to have a lower forced expiratory volume (the volume of air you are able to take in and forcibly exhale in one second) after middle age because of changes in muscles and stiffening of chest walls. This decreased lung function may cause doctors to miss the diagnosis of adult-onset asthma.

Diagnosing adult-onset asthma

Your asthma doctor may diagnose adult-onset asthma by:

- Taking a medical history, asking about symptoms, and listening to you breathe
- Performing a lung function test, using a device called a spirometer, to measure how much air you can exhale after first taking a deep breath and how fast you can empty your lungs. You may be asked before or after the test to inhale a short-acting bronchodilator (medicine that opens the airways by relaxing tight muscles and that also help clear mucus from the lungs).

Performing a methacholine challenge test

This asthma test may be performed if your symptoms and spirometry test do not clearly show asthma. When inhaled, methacholine causes the airways to spasm and narrow if asthma is present. During this test, you inhale increasing amounts of methacholine aerosol mist before and after spirometry. The methacholine test is considered positive, meaning asthma is present, if the lung function drops by at least 20%. A bronchodilator is always given at the end of the test to reverse the effects of the methacholine.

Performing a chest X-ray

An X-ray is an image of the body that is created by using low doses of radiation reflected on special film or a fluorescent screen. X-rays can be used to diagnose a wide range of conditions, from bronchitis to a broken bone. Your doctor might perform an X-ray exam on you in order to see the structures inside your chest, including the heart, lungs, and bones. By viewing your lungs, your doctor can see if you have a condition other than asthma that may account for your symptoms. Although there may be signs on an X-ray that suggest asthma, a person with asthma will often have a normal chest X-ray.

Childhood asthma (discussed further in chapter 5).

(See diagram overleaf)

In childhood asthma, the lungs and airways become easily inflamed when exposed to certain triggers, such as inhaling pollen or catching a cold or other respiratory infection. Childhood asthma can cause bothersome daily symptoms that interfere with play, sports, school and sleep. In some children, unmanaged asthma can cause dangerous asthma attacks.

Childhood asthma isn't a different condition from asthma in adults, but children face unique challenges. The condition is a leading cause of emergency department visits, hospitalizations and missed school days. Unfortunately, childhood asthma can't be cured, and symptoms can continue into adulthood. But with the right treatment, you and your child can keep symptoms under control and prevent damage to growing lungs.

Seasonal asthma

If you only experience asthma symptoms at certain times of the year, you could have seasonal asthma. You may find that your asthma gets worse when it's very cold, or when there's pollen in the air. Asthma is a long-term condition, even if you don't experience your symptoms all year round. If you think you have asthma, see your doctor, who will devise a treatment plan.

Winter

According to Asthma UK, 75 per cent of people report that cold air triggers their asthma symptoms. Some people find that just breathing in very cold air causes symptoms. When the air hits the airways it can sometimes make them go into spasm, which causes coughing, wheezing, a tight chest and breathlessness.

Spring

Around 50 per cent of people with asthma also have allergies, and if that's you, you could find that the extra pollen in the air at this time of year aggravates or sets off your asthma. Seasonal pollen in springtime can cause inflammation in your airways and make underlying allergic asthma worse.

Summer

For some people, very hot weather triggers their asthma symptoms - it's thought that the hot air can cause the airways to narrow, just like very cold air does. It's also possible that the amount of pollutants and mould in the air increase as it gets hotter.

Autumn

Change of weather generally and thunderstorms are also known to cause serious asthma attacks for some people - they lead to a six-fold increase in hospital admissions for asthma. It's not known exactly why this is, although the theory is that it's linked to high levels of humidity in the air, plus pollen and mould particles being swept up and broken down by the windy conditions that often accompany a storm, and then scattered back down where they are breathed in.

How can you prevent seasonal asthma?

If you know that a change in the weather or certain weather conditions make your symptoms worse, it's advisable to always keep a close eye on weather, pollen and pollution forecasts so that you're prepared. It also helps to keep your asthma well managed and make sure that you have a written asthma plan which is up to date.

Take your medication as advised.

Make sure that you attend regular check-ups with your GP.

How to prevent asthma in cold, damp weather:

- Keep your reliever inhaler with you.
- Make sure you use your preventer inhaler if your doctor has prescribed one.
- Keep an eye on your symptoms; if you need to use your reliever more often, you need to speak to your doctor.
- Keep as warm and dry as possible.
- When you go out in the cold, wear a scarf over your mouth and nose to help warm the air.
- Try breathing in through your nose instead of your mouth, as this helps warm the air.

How to prevent hot weather triggering your asthma:

- Keep your reliever inhaler with you.

- Make sure you use your preventer inhaler if your doctor has prescribed one
- Don't leave your inhalers lying around in direct sunlight or anywhere they might get too hot like a parked car.
- Make sure you're managing your hay fever well too, as hay fever symptoms can make asthma worse.
- Don't exercise outdoors between 11am and 3pm.
- If you plan to go outside, try to go out earlier in the day to make the most of better air quality.
- Drink plenty of water.
- Keep doors and windows closed while you're indoors.

How to stop spring pollen from triggering an asthma attack:
Keep your reliever inhaler with you.
- Make sure you use your preventer inhaler if your doctor has prescribed one
- Keep an eye on the pollen forecast, either on TV or with an app on your phone/tablet.
- Avoid going outside when pollen is at its highest if you can. This is normally between 5am and 10am.
- Shower and wash your clothes after going outside.
- Dry your sheets and clothes indoors.
- If you have it, use air conditioning instead of open windows in your car (and indoors).
- Keep your grass short, if possible, and if you can get someone else to look after it for you!

- Exercise indoors wherever possible. If you have to work out outside, take your asthma medications before you go.

Avoiding thunderstorm related asthma symptoms:
- Keep an eye on the weather forecast or download an app that can tell you when storms are approaching.
- If a storm is forecast, get indoors as soon as you can and stay indoors before, during and after the storm with the windows closed.
- Shower and change your clothes if you've been outside, to get rid of any pollen.
- Keep your reliever close by.
- If you have hay fever, take your usual medicine.
- Don't smoke or let other people smoke around you
- Make sure that you know what to do if your symptoms get worse, and how to recognise when they do.

****

Part 3:

The Home and Asthma

Chapter 3

Asthma Triggers Within the Home

House Dust Mites

Dust mites are microscopic arachnids that live all over your house, including on pillows, toys, linens, furniture, blankets, and elsewhere. Despite how small they are, dust mites leave lots of droppings, and these droppings can trigger allergic and asthmatic reactions. House mite allergy is a hypersensitive reaction to proteins in the excrement of dust mites. These proteins can cause an allergic reaction in the respiratory passages causing the symptoms of hay fever and asthma. It can often aggravate atopic dermatitis (eczema) in people who have this problem, causing facial eczema that can be difficult to treat.

Unlike pollen, dust mites are present all year round causing constant allergy – 'perennial' allergic rhinitis. The excretion from the mites dries out and can be launched into the air when someone hoovers, walks over a rug, sits down in a chair, moves on the mattress, or shakes the bed clothes, giving allergic people immediate symptoms.

Symptoms of house dust mite allergy
- Hay fever like symptoms: runny nose, itching, sneezing.
- Watering itchy eyes.
- Asthma, coughing, difficulty in breathing.
- Eczema (inflammatory skin disease) may get worse.
- Air pollution such as tobacco smoke, chemical irritants, or car fumes.

You can reduce the incidence of house dust mites, although not eliminate them altogether. The following are basic tips on the actions you can take.

Cleaning your house
- **Dust with a damp cloth.** Dust mites feed on dead skin, dander, and other things that are found in dust. Therefore, where there's dust, there are likely dust mites.

■ A key to eliminating dust mites is getting rid of their food source, and that means dusting with a damp cloth. Rinse the cloth regularly to avoid spreading dust. It's important to use a damp cloth because a dry cloth will just stir up allergens and spread dust around the house.

Items to dust include furniture, shelves, books, decorations, trinkets, pictures, fixtures, and other items that collect dust.

■ **Vacuum the entire house.** Vacuuming is another great way to get rid of dust, skin, dust mite feaces, and other allergens from your house. To avoid spreading dust and allergens, it's important that you use a vacuum outfitted with a HEPA filter that will trap allergens and prevent them from being blown around the house.

■ When vacuuming, pay particular attention to floors, baseboards, furniture, carpeting, rugs, and behind and underneath furniture. Use upholstery attachments to get the seams, crevices, and corners of your furniture.

■ **Wash your bedding in hot water.** Dust mites can be found all over your bedding. Remove the pillowcases, sheets, blankets, and covers from your bed. Place the items in the washing machine and wash them with hot water and the regular cycle. When the washing machine is done, transfer the items to the dryer and dry them on a hot setting.

- **To kill dust mites**, the washing machine or dryer must reach between 130 and 140 F (54 to 60 C).
- **Clean curtains and drapes.** Dust mites love heavy curtains as much as they love pillows and bedding. Remove curtains and drapes from their rods or tracks and check the care label for washing instructions.
- For washable curtains, remove any hooks or hangers. Transfer the curtains to the washing machine and wash them with hot water. Transfer them to the dryer or hang them to dry according to the care label. Some curtains may be dry clean only. Take the curtains to a dry cleaner to kill dust mites.
- **Wash toys.** Toys, stuffed animals, and other fabric items are great hiding places for dust mites. Collect all washable items and wash them in the washing machine using hot water. Transfer the load to the dryer and dry the items on high heat.
- Freeze items that can't be washed. There are some items that you won't be able to machine wash to kill dust mites. With these items, you can freeze them instead to get rid of mites. Transfer each item to a separate plastic bag and seal the bag tightly. Transfer the item to the freezer and leave it there for 24 hours.

- Good candidates for freezing include:
- Pillows

- Special toys
- Delicate fabrics

Creating an anti-dust mite environment

It is very important to try to reduce humidity levels in the house. Dust mites love high humidity. The easiest way to decrease the humidity in your house is with a dehumidifier. You can also decrease the humidity by opening windows on dry days. Always use fans and vents when cooking, showering, and other activities that create steam. By reducing the humidity in your house, you can create an environment that's not ideal for dust mites, and you will slow down how quickly they reproduce. Install a hygrometer to keep an eye on the humidity and keep the level below 50 percent.

Turn down the temperature.

Dust mites also love high temperatures. The ideal temperature for them is between 75 and 80 F (24 and 27 C). In winter, set your thermostat to 70 F (21 C), and even cooler in the bedroom if that's comfortable. In summer, use fans, windows, and air conditioning when necessary to keep your house cooler.

Spray your home with a disinfecting spray.

Disinfectants are ideal for killing dust mites and will make your home inhospitable to them. After your regular dusting, spray the disinfecting spray everywhere that dust tends to collect, including:

- Corners
- Baseboards
- Floors
- Shelves
- Curtains
- Near furniture

Use eucalyptus.

Certain essential oils, and eucalyptus specifically, are effective at killing dust mites. There are a few ways you can use eucalyptus around the house to make your home unfriendly for dust mites, including:

- Add 20 drops of eucalyptus oil to your washing machine, especially when you're using a cold or warm water setting.
- Pour about 30 drops of eucalyptus oil into a spray bottle and fill the bottle with water. Use the spray around the house, including on your bed, furniture, pillows, toys, carpets, and other areas where dust mites live.

Controlling dust mites

Get rid of clutter.

Clutter and unnecessary items around the house attract and trap dust, and this creates a feeding frenzy for dust mites. One of the best ways to get rid of dust mites is to eliminate their food source, and while it's not possible to completely get rid of dust, you can reduce it by throwing out, selling, or properly storing items like:

- Books
- Decorations and ornaments
- Picture frames
- Trinkets
- Home accessories
- Decorative pillows

Dust regularly.

Regular dusting with a damp cloth is a great way to reduce dust in the house and eliminate food sources for dust mites. Always dust by wiping surfaces with a damp cloth to avoid spreading dust and other allergens around the house. For the best results, dust your entire house on a weekly basis.

Wash linens and bedding regularly.

Because linens and bedding are such a hot spot for dust mites, it's important to keep these clean. Weekly washing in hot water that's between 130 and 140 F (54 to 60 C) will help to control dust mites in your bedroom. Be sure to wash:

- Sheets
- Pillowcases
- Duvet covers
- Blankets

Get rid of carpeting.

Carpets and rugs are among the worst places in your house for harbouring dust mites. While regular vacuuming and washing (for small rugs) will help to reduce mite numbers, getting rid of the carpet altogether will be even more effective. When possible, remove carpeting and replace it with:

- Tile
- Hardwood
- Laminate
- Cork
- Concrete

Replace dust-collecting fabrics with easy-to-clean items.
Because things like thick curtains and drapes can house large numbers of dust mites, you can help get rid of them by replacing these items. For instance, you can replace curtains with plastic blinds or wooden shutters, and fabric cushions and pillows with leather ones. Not only are these items easier to clean, but they also won't attract dust mites the way fabrics do.

Groom pets regularly.
Pet dander is another huge food source for dust mites. To reduce dander in the house, take your dogs and cats outside daily for a thorough brushing.

For dogs, you should also give them monthly baths to reduce dander and fur around the house. Pets can also suffer from dust mite allergies, so keeping them cleaner is beneficial for you both.

Use mattress and pillow covers.

Mattress and pillow covers are plastic or hypoallergenic fabric envelopes that protect your bed from dust mites, bed bugs, and allergens. The covers encase your mattress or pillows and prevent dust mites from getting in, and protect you from allergens that are already present. To keep these covers clean, wipe plastic ones with a damp cloth and wash fabric ones weekly.

Increase the ventilation in your house.

Better ventilation means lower humidity, more airflow, and less dust, and all of these are good for controlling dust mites. You can improve ventilation by opening windows, using ceiling and portable fans, and by making use of vents in the house, such as in the kitchen and bathroom.

Finally, don't allow smoking in your house under any circumstances!

Medicine available for dust mite allergies

Medicines for allergies include:

- Antihistamine tablets or syrup (e.g. loratadine, cetirizine). These lessen the allergic reaction by blocking the actions of histamine. They relieve hay fever type symptoms.
- Nasal sprays or drops containing sodium cromoglicate, corticosteroids (e.g. beclometasone) or antihistamines (e.g. levocabastine). These can be used to reduce nasal inflammation and control symptoms in the nose.
- Eye drops containing sodium cromoglicate, nedocromil, or antihistamines (e.g., azelastine) reduce eye inflammation and can be used if eye symptoms are a particular problem.

If the allergy causes asthmatic symptoms, some of the asthma medication below may be used.

- Relievers (bronchodilators): these are quick-acting medicines that relax the muscles of the airways. They are used when required to relieve shortness of breath. If used regularly more than three times weekly, a preventer is needed.
- Preventers: these act over a longer time and work by reducing the inflammation within the airways. They should be used regularly for maximum benefit. When the dosage and type of preventive medicine is correct, there will be little need for reliever medicines.

Relievers

There are three groups of bronchodilators.

Beta-2 agonists

Beta-2 agonists cause the airways to relax and widen. Examples of those which act for a short time (3 or 4 hours following a single dose) are salbutamol and terbutaline. These medicines are inhaled from a variety of delivery devices, the most familiar being the pressurised metered-dose-inhaler (MDI). When inhaled, these types of medicines work within minutes to open the airways, making breathing easier.

Longer-acting beta-2 agonists include salmeterol and formoterol. Their action lasts over 12 hours, making them suitable for twice daily dosage to keep the airways open.

Anticholinergics

One of the ways in which the size of the airways is naturally controlled is through nerves that connect to the muscles surrounding the airways. The nerve impulses cause the muscles to contract, thus narrowing the airway. Anticholinergic medicines such as ipratropium block this effect, allowing the airways to open. The size of this effect is fairly small, so it is most noticeable if the airways have already been narrowed by other conditions, such as chronic bronchitis.

Theophyllines and aminophylline

Theophylline and aminophylline are given by mouth and are less commonly used in Britain because they are more likely to produce side effects than inhaled treatment. They are still in very wide use throughout the world. All three types of reliever can be combined if necessary.

Preventers

Below are the main groups of anti-inflammatories.

- **Corticosteroids**

Corticosteroids (or 'steroids') work to reduce the amount of inflammation within the airways, reducing their tendency to contract. They are usually given as inhaled treatment, e.g., fluticasone or triamcinolone, although sometimes oral steroid tablets may be required for severe attacks. Although steroid tablets are powerful medicines with many potential side effects, when inhaled in microscopic doses for asthma their safety has been well established. It is also important to balance the problems that arise from poorly treated asthma against the improvement in health which occurs when the condition is well treated.

- **Leukotriene receptor antagonists**

Leukotriene receptor antagonists are compounds released by inflammatory cells within the lungs and which have a powerful constricting effect upon the airways. By blocking this effect with these antagonist medicines, the constriction is reversed. There are two such medicines currently available: montelukast and zafirlukast.

Most cases of allergic asthma are best controlled with an inhaled corticosteroid, e.g. fluticasone or budesonide, which is taken at regular intervals as a preventative measure. A beta-2 agonist, e.g. salbutamol, is used in conjunction with this to relieve symptoms when necessary, however some patients respond very well to leukotriene receptor antagonists. A trial of 2-4 months can be instituted to assess for efficacy.

****

Part 4: The Different Types of medication Available

Chapter 4

Asthma Medication and Treatments

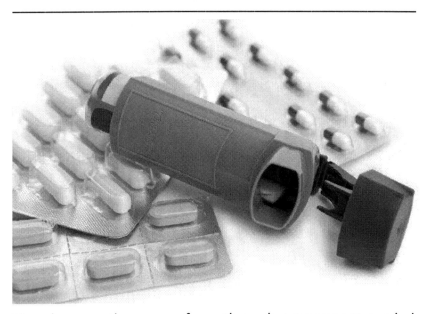

There's currently no cure for asthma, but treatment can help control the symptoms so you're able to live a normal, active life.

Inhalers – devices that let you breathe in medicine – are the main treatment. Tablets and other treatments may also be needed if your asthma is severe. You'll usually create a personal action plan with your doctor or asthma nurse. This includes information about your medicines, how to monitor your condition and what to do if you have an asthma attack.

Inhalers

Inhalers can help:

- relieve symptoms when they occur (reliever inhalers)
- stop symptoms developing (preventer inhalers)
- Some people need an inhaler that does both (combination inhalers).

Reliever inhalers

Most people with asthma will be given a reliever inhaler. These are usually blue. You use a reliever inhaler to treat your symptoms when they occur. They should relieve your symptoms within a few minutes. Tell your GP or asthma nurse if you must use your reliever inhaler 3 or more times a week.

They may suggest additional treatment, such as a preventer inhaler.

Reliever inhalers have few side effects, but they can sometimes cause shaking or a fast heartbeat for a few minutes after they're used.

Preventer inhalers

If you need to use a reliever inhaler often, you may also need a preventer inhaler. You use a preventer inhaler every day to reduce the inflammation and sensitivity of your airways, which stops your symptoms occurring. It's important to use it even when you do not have symptoms. Speak to your GP or asthma nurse if you continue to have symptoms while using a preventer inhaler. Preventer inhalers contain steroid medicine. They do not usually have side effects, but can sometimes cause:

- a fungal infection of the mouth or throat (oral thrush)
- a hoarse voice
- a sore throat

You can help prevent these side effects by using a spacer, which is a hollow plastic tube you attach to your inhaler, as well as by rinsing your mouth or cleaning your teeth after using your inhaler.

Combination inhalers

If using reliever and preventer inhalers does not control your asthma, you may need an inhaler that combines both. Combination inhalers are used every day to help stop symptoms occurring and provide long-lasting relief if they do occur. It's important to use it regularly, even if you do not have symptoms. Side effects of combination inhalers are similar to those of reliever and preventer inhalers.

Tablets

You may also need to take tablets if using an inhaler alone is not helping control your symptoms.

Leukotriene receptor antagonists (LTRAs)

LTRAs are the main tablets used for asthma. They also come in syrup and powder form. You take them every day to help stop your symptoms occurring. Possible side effects include tummy aches and headaches.

Theophylline

Theophylline may also be recommended if other treatments are not helping to control your symptoms. It's taken every day to stop your symptoms occurring. Possible side effects include headaches and feeling sick.

Steroid tablets

Steroid tablets may be recommended if other treatments are not helping to control your symptoms. They can be taken either:

- as an immediate treatment when you have an asthma attack
- every day as a long-term treatment to prevent symptoms – this is usually only necessary if you have very severe asthma and inhalers do not control your symptoms.
- Long-term or frequent use of steroid tablets can occasionally cause side effects such as:
- increased appetite, leading to weight gain.
- easy bruising
- mood changes
- fragile bones (osteoporosis)
- high blood pressure

You'll be monitored regularly while taking steroid tablets to check for signs of any problems.

Other treatments

Other treatments, such as injections or surgery, are rarely needed, but may be recommended if all other treatments are not helping.

Injections

For some people with severe asthma, injections given every few weeks can help control the symptoms. The main injections for asthma are:

- benralizumab (Fasenra)
- omalizumab (Xolair)
- mepolizumab (Nucala)
- reslizumab (Cinqaero)

These medicines are not suitable for everyone with asthma and can only be prescribed by an asthma specialist. The main side effect is discomfort where the injection is given.

Surgery

A procedure called bronchial thermoplasty may be offered as a treatment for severe asthma. It works well and there are no serious concerns about its safety. You will be sedated or put to sleep using a general anaesthetic during a bronchial thermoplasty. It involves passing a thin, flexible tube down your throat and into your lungs. Heat is then used on the muscles around the airways to help stop them narrowing and causing asthma symptoms.

Complementary therapies

Several complementary therapies have been suggested as possible treatments for asthma, including:

- breathing exercises – such as techniques called the Papworth method and the Buteyko method
- traditional Chinese herbal medicine
- acupuncture
- ionisers – devices that use an electric current to charge molecules of air
- manual therapies – such as chiropractic
- homeopathy
- dietary supplements

There's some evidence that breathing exercises can improve symptoms and reduce the need for reliever medicines in some people, but they shouldn't be used instead of your medicine.

****

Part 5: Asthma in Children

Chapter 5

Childhood Asthma

What Is Childhood Asthma?

Childhood asthma is the same disease adults get, but it affects children differently. Your child's lungs and airways can easily get inflamed when they're exposed to things like pollen or a cold. The symptoms may only make it hard for your child to play outside, take part in sports, or sleep. But sometimes they can cause dangerous asthma attacks that result in a trip to the hospital. Childhood asthma isn't curable, but you can work with your child's doctor to treat it and prevent damage to their growing lungs.

Signs and Symptoms of Asthma in children

Not all children have the same asthma symptoms, and they can vary from episode to episode in the same child. Possible signs and symptoms of asthma in children include:

- Frequent coughing spells, which can happen during play, at night, or while laughing or crying
- A chronic cough (which may be the only symptom)
- Less energy during play
- Rapid breathing (from time to time)
- Complaint of chest tightness or chest hurting
- Wheezing -- a whistling sound when breathing in or out
- Retractions -- seesaw motions in the chest from laboured breathing
- Shortness of breath, loss of breath
- Tightened neck and chest muscles
- Feeling weak or tired

While these are some signs, your child's doctor should check out any illness that makes it hard for her to breathe. A doctor might use terms like reactive airways disease or bronchiolitis when describing episodes of wheezing with shortness of breath or cough in infants and toddlers (even though these illnesses usually respond to asthma medications). Tests to confirm asthma may not be accurate until after age five.

.

Causes and Triggers of Childhood Asthma

Common triggers include:

- Airway infections: Colds, pneumonia, sinus infections
- Allergens: Things your child is allergic to, like cockroaches, dust mites, mould, pet dander, pollen
- Irritants: Things that bother the airways like air pollution, chemicals, cold air, odours, smoke
- Exercise: It can lead to wheezing, coughing, and a tight chest.
- Stress: It can make your child feel short of breath and worsen their symptoms.

How Is Asthma Diagnosed in Children?

By the time you get your child into the doctor's office, their asthma symptoms may be gone. That means you are key in helping the doctor understand what's going on. When you see the doctor, you can expect:

- Questions about medical history and asthma symptoms: The doctor will ask about any history of breathing problems you or your child may have had, as well as any family history of asthma, allergies, a skin condition called eczema, or other lung disease. It's important that you describe your child's symptoms -- coughing, wheezing, shortness of breath, chest pain, or tightness -- in detail, including when and how often they happen.

- Physical exam: During the physical exam, the doctor will listen to your child's heart and lungs and look for signs of an allergic nose or eyes.

- Tests: Your child might get a chest X-ray. If they are 6 or older, they may take a simple test to see how well the lungs work called spirometry. It measures the amount of air in the lungs and how fast they can blow it out. This helps the doctor find out how severe the asthma is. Other tests can help find asthma triggers. They may include allergy skin testing, blood tests (IgE or RAST), and X-rays to find out if sinus infections or gastroesophageal reflux disease (GERD) is making the asthma worse. A test that measures the level of nitric oxide (eNO) in her breath can also point to inflamed airways.

How Common Is Asthma in Children?

Asthma is the leading cause of chronic illness in children and, for unknown reasons, is steadily increasing. Asthma can begin at any age (even in the elderly), but most children have their first symptoms by age 5. Many things can make childhood asthma more likely:

- Nasal allergies (hay fever) or eczema (allergic skin rash)
- A family history of asthma or allergies
- Frequent respiratory infections
- Low birth weight
- Exposure to tobacco smoke before or after birth
- Black or Puerto Rican ethnicity
- Being raised in a low-income environment

How Is Asthma Treated in Children?

Avoiding triggers, using medications, and keeping an eye on daily asthma symptoms are the ways to control asthma in children of all ages. Keep them away from all sources of smoke. As we have discussed previously, there are two main types of asthma medications:

- Quick-relief medications help with sudden symptoms. Your child will take them for fast help during an asthma attack.

- Long-acting medications work to prevent airway inflammation and keep your child's asthma under control. Your child will probably take them every day.

Based on your child's history and how bad their asthma is, the doctor will come up with an asthma action plan and give you a written copy. This plan describes when and how the child should use asthma drugs, what to do when asthma gets worse, and when to seek emergency care. Make sure you understand this plan and ask the doctor any questions you may have.

Your child's written asthma action plan is key to controlling their asthma. Keep it handy to remind you of the daily management plan and as a guide when they get asthma symptoms. Make sure the child's teachers have copies so they'll know how to treat the symptoms if the child has an asthma attack away from home.

Note that many of these medications contain steroids, which have side effects. They can irritate your child's mouth and throat in the short term. Over a long period, they may stunt growth and lead to a bone problem like osteoporosis, reduced blood supply to the bones, and cataracts. They might make your child's body less able to make natural steroids. But untreated asthma can lead to hospital visits, so you and your doctor should weigh the pros and cons when creating an asthma action plan.

When to Go to Accident and Emergency

Your child needs emergency care for a severe asthma attack. Watch for these signs:

- Stopping in mid-sentence to catch a breath
- Using their stomach muscles to breathe
- Their abdomen sinks in under their ribs when they try to get air.
- Their chest and side pull in as they breathe.
- Their nostrils widen.
- Their heartbeat races
- They sweat.
- They have chest pain.

How Do I Give Asthma Drugs to a Toddler?

Infants and toddlers may use some of the same types of asthma drugs as older children and adults. Inhaled steroids can be key to managing infants with chronic asthma or wheezing. Children under 4 may get lower doses and take their medications through an asthma nebulizer. This device changes the medicine from a liquid to a mist that your child breathes in through a face mask. The doctor will tell you how often to give these breathing treatments, but it's usually up to four times a day, about 10-15 minutes at a time. To use the nebulizer:

- Wash your hands.
- Place the medicine in the nebulizer.
- Connect the tubes from the compressor to the base.

- Attach the mouthpiece.
- Turn the compressor on and look for a light mist to come from the nebulizer.
- Put the mouthpiece in your child's mouth and have them close their lips around it.
- Have them breathe in until their treatment time is up.
- Turn the nebulizer off when the medicine is gone.
- Have your child cough to clear any mucus.

The latest asthma guidelines have steps for managing asthma in children up to age 4. This includes the use of quick-relief medications (like albuterol) for off-and-on asthma symptoms. A low dose of an inhaled steroid, cromolyn, or Singulair is the next step up. Then the focus shifts from symptom control to disease management. If you can control children's asthma for at least 3 months, the doctor may lower, or step down, the asthma treatment. He/she will talk to you about exact medications and dosages.

Younger children will probably take inhaled asthma drugs or liquid medications with a nebulizer. Older children may be able to use a metered dose inhaler (MDI) with a spacer. A spacer is a chamber that attaches to the MDI and holds the burst of medication. This lets your child breathe the medication into their lungs at their own pace.

To use an inhaler with a spacer:

- Wash your hands.

- Prime the inhaler the first time you use it by spraying it 4 times into the air.
- Put the inhaler into the opening at the end of the spacer.
- Shake it for 10 seconds.
- Have your child turn their head to the side and breathe out.
- Have them close their mouth around the mouthpiece of the spacer.
- Tell them to take a slow deep breath.
- Make them hold it in and count to 10.
- Have them slowly breathe out.

If your doctor prescribes two puffs of medicine, wait 1 minute after the first puff, then do it all again.

What Are the Goals of Treating My Child's Asthma?

Asthma can't be cured, but it can be controlled. If your child can't meet all these goals, contact the child's doctor for advice. The child should be able to:

- Live an active, normal life
- Prevent chronic and troublesome symptoms
- Attend school every day
- Avoid asthma symptoms during the night
- Do daily activities, play, and engage in sports without difficulty
- Stop the need for urgent visits to the doctor, emergency department, or hospital

- Use and adjust medications to control asthma with little or no side effects

By learning about asthma and how to control it, you take an important step toward managing your child's asthma. Work closely with her asthma care team to learn all you can about asthma, how to avoid asthma triggers, what asthma drugs do, and how to correctly give asthma treatments.

Will My Child Outgrow Asthma?

Much is unknown about infant lung function and asthma. But experts believe that a child is more likely to be diagnosed with asthma after the age of 7 if they have had multiple wheezing episodes, has a mother with asthma, or has allergies. Also, once their airways become sensitive, they remain that way for life. But about 50% of children see a sharp drop in asthma symptoms once they reach their teens. It may seem they've outgrown their asthma, but some will have symptoms again as adults. Unfortunately, there's no way to predict who will be affected.

Why Is Childhood Asthma on the Rise?

No one really knows the exact reasons why more and more children are getting asthma. Some experts suggest that children spend too much time indoors with dust, air pollution, and second-hand smoke. Others say children aren't exposed to enough childhood illnesses to help their immune systems learn to fight bacteria and viruses.

****

Part 6:

Diet and Asthma

Chapter 6

Diet and Asthma

Childhood asthma is a significant health problem as we have seen. Although the relationship between nutrition and asthma is still being established, there is little doubt that a healthy diet can have an impact on asthma. There is no single diet recommended for children/adults with asthma, but the so-called Mediterranean diet -- low in saturated fats, rich in fruits and vegetables, and high in fibre -- has been associated with reduced asthma symptoms. Understanding good nutrition and potential dietary influences on your child's and your own asthma can be an important part of your overall strategy for symptom control.

Plant Foods

Eating lots of fruits and vegetables is associated with better respiratory health and improved asthma symptoms in children. Past studies have found a link between antioxidants and other nutrients in fresh fruits and vegetables and better lung function and fewer asthma symptoms.

Specifically, a high consumption rate of apples and pears was linked to less tightening of the airways, or broncho-reactivity, in a study of young adults. Nuts and seeds rich in flavonoids and other compounds with antioxidant effects help fight inflammation, which may boost respiratory health. In particular, carrots could also protect against exercise-induced asthma. That's because they're loaded with beta-carotene, an antioxidant that's converted to vitamin A in the body, which boosts the immune system against asthma attacks. The more vivid the colour of the carrot, the higher the levels of this important carotenoid.

Drink milk

Not only is milk a great source of calcium, but it is also rich in magnesium, an asthma-fighting mineral also found in flax seeds. Magnesium relaxes the muscles surrounding the bronchi, which keeps your airways open.

Fish

Fish can be a good source of omega-3 fatty acids and is considered part of a healthy diet. With respect to respiratory conditions of childhood, studies of fish consumption have had contradictory findings -- some suggesting positive effects, and some suggesting no improvement or even worsening of asthma. Generally, fish provides an abundance of vitamins and minerals, in addition to being rich in omega-3s, all thought to have beneficial effects on inflammatory disorders and lung function. The benefits might even begin before birth: one study at the University of Southampton found that children whose mothers ate salmon twice a week while pregnant were less likely to develop asthma.

Fibre

In a study of 1,921 adults published in the January 2016 issue of "Annals of the American Thoracic Society," low fibre intake was associated with diminished lung function, while a diet rich in fibre was associated with healthy respiratory function. Fibre has anti-inflammatory properties and may help guard against allergic diseases such as asthma. Dietary fibre also contains prebiotics -- nutrients that help "feed" or promote the growth of good bacteria in the gut, some of which may help fight inflammation.

Therefore, whole grains like brown rice and legumes like lentils and pinto beans are recommended as part of a healthy diet.

*

Foods That Are Bad for Asthma

Just as important as consuming fresh, nutrient-rich foods is avoiding unhealthy choices. Fast food and particularly fast-food hamburgers have been associated with a higher prevalence of asthma flare-ups. Reasons for the association are unclear, but it's possible industrial processing, hydrogenated vegetable fats and trans-fatty acids may be to blame; meat consumption in general is not believed to be a contributing factor to asthma. Drinks sweetened with high fructose corn syrup have been linked to asthma in children and students. Beverages with excess free fructose (EFF) -- which includes apple juice, drinks with high fructose corn syrup and soft drinks -- have also been linked to asthma in children.

Excess Weight and Managing Asthma

Proper asthma control requires working with your child's doctor, but healthy eating at home is important in more ways than one. Excess weight and obesity may result when there is a mismatch between calories consumed and calories spent. Excess weight, in addition to poor nutrition, is increasingly recognized as risky for health in general -- and for asthma, specifically. Obesity has been linked to decreased efficacy of inhaled corticosteroids, which are often prescribed for asthma. Asthmatic children who are also overweight are encouraged to lose weight.

Food allergies

If you have asthma and a food allergy, you're more at risk of having an asthma attack that's life threatening. Food could be an asthma trigger for you because you're:

- allergic to certain foods. This means you can have an allergic reaction very quickly when you encounter your food allergen. And the allergic reaction quickly brings on your asthma symptoms such as wheezing, coughing and difficulty breathing. People with food allergies need to strictly avoid the food they react to.

- sensitive to certain foods, or additives in foods, such as preservatives. Being sensitive to certain foods is not the same as a true allergy, and there's less clear-cut evidence to show a link to asthma symptoms. But some people with asthma tell us that other kinds of chemicals and ingredients in food products trigger their asthma symptoms.

How do you know food is one of your asthma triggers?

Although a lot of food allergies start in childhood, you can develop them as an adult too. If you think food might be bringing on your asthma symptoms, but you're not sure, talk to your GP or asthma nurse soon. Evidence shows that an asthma attack that's triggered by an allergic reaction to food can be worse, particularly for children with food allergies.

Children with food allergies and asthma are more likely to have high risk allergic reactions to food. This means they're more likely to have possibly fatal anaphylactic reactions, particularly if their asthma isn't well controlled. Your GP can:

- Help you work out how to keep a food diary to identify patterns and clues about which foods might be affecting you, or your child. This might include writing down what you eat each day, and any asthma symptoms.

- Offer you a referral for skin prick testing to help confirm or rule out any food allergies.

- Discuss possible food sensitivities with you – which won't show up in an allergy test.

- Support you in excluding certain foods or food groups if you need to, to see if symptoms improve.

- Help you work out if it's something else, for example acid reflux, that's making your asthma symptoms worse, rather than an allergy

- Update your written asthma action plan and talk about the best ways to deal with any asthma symptoms triggered by food.

How to avoid food triggering asthma symptoms or an asthma attack

If you have a food allergy and asthma there are five things you need to do to cut your risk of an asthma attack.

- Avoid the foods you're allergic to

- If you have an auto-injector, keep it with you. Use this immediately if you're having severe anaphylactic symptoms.
- Always keep your asthma reliever inhaler with you, to use if food triggers your asthma symptoms.
- Use your preventer inhaler every day to control inflammation in your airways, meaning you're less likely to react badly to your asthma triggers. If you have a food allergy, and your asthma's not well controlled, it increases your risk of any allergic reaction being more severe.
- Talk to your GP or asthma nurse and get your written asthma action plan updated with any new trigger's information. It's important that you manage your asthma and your food allergy together to cut the risk of one making the other worse.

What are the most common food allergies or sensitivities?
Although any kind of food may cause a sensitivity or allergy in some people, there are some food types that are much more likely to cause a problem. Some of the most common food allergens are:
- gluten (from wheat and cereal products)
- shellfish
- eggs
- milk
- tree nuts

- peanuts
- sesame seeds and soya.

Some food allergies, such as allergies to milk and eggs, are more common in children. The most common food sensitivities that can trigger asthma symptoms are:

- Histamine – this is a naturally produced ingredient in some foods such as yogurt, mature cheese, and smoked meats. It's also found in alcoholic drinks like wine.
- Sulphites – these are used as preservatives in foods such as processed meats and pickled foods. They're also found in drinks such as wine, beer and cider.

How to cut the risk of food triggering asthma symptoms

- Get 'free from' lists from your local supermarket. These will show you all the products free from the allergen you have to avoid.
- Avoid ready meals. If you prepare your own meals, you'll feel more confident about what's gone into them.
- Plan ahead for eating out. Call ahead to make sure all restaurant staff, from the chef to the kitchen staff, to the waiters know about your allergy.
- Read labels carefully. By law the 14 major allergens (including wheat, milk, nuts and egg) have to be clearly listed in bold on pre-packed manufactured foods throughout the EU. If you're allergic, or sensitive, to

ingredients outside of this list you'll need to read the whole list through to check. Check and double check because it may not be immediately obvious that your trigger ingredient is in a product.

****

Part 7:

Exercise and Asthma

Chapter 7

Exercise and Asthma

Exercise and physical activity are vital for keeping fit and healthy and are an important part of good asthma management. Sometimes, however, exercising or being physically active can trigger an episode of asthma. This is called exercise-induced asthma (EIA). It is also known as exercise-induced bronchoconstriction (EIB) and both terms are often used. Exercise-induced asthma is usually easily managed and should be part of any asthma management plan. In fact, regular exercise will improve your overall health and well-being. You should be able to exercise as often as you wish. If you regularly experience asthma symptoms during exercise, consult your doctor or respiratory specialist.

People with asthma should be able to participate in almost any sport or exercise. Scuba diving is the only sport not recommended. Most people with asthma can exercise to their full potential if they have good asthma control. Many top athletes who have competed at the national and international level have asthma.

Exercise-induced asthma

When resting, you normally breathe through your nose, which warms and moistens the air travelling to your lungs. During exercise and physical activity, you will often breathe more quickly through your mouth, causing cold and dry air to travel to your lungs, irritating the airways. The cold and dry air can cause the muscles around the airway to tighten, increasing the chance of experiencing an asthma flare-up. Shortness of breath during or after physical activity is common. However, if physical activity causes symptoms with no relief after rest, you may have exercise-induced asthma. Those symptoms include:

- shortness of breath
- feeling of a tight chest
- dry or persistent cough
- wheeze.

If you experience asthma symptoms during physical activity or exercise, consult your doctor for further advice.

Tips to help prevent exercise-induced asthma

To prevent exercise-induced asthma, suggestions include:

- Make sure that your asthma is being well managed, as this will make exercise-induced asthma less likely to occur.
- Always carry your reliever medication and spacer with you.
- If written on your Asthma Action Plan, take your reliever medication up to 15 minutes before warming up.
- Warm up before exercise as usual.

During exercise, watch for asthma symptoms and stop and take your reliever medication if symptoms appear. Only return to exercise if your asthma symptoms have been relieved. If asthma symptoms appear for a second time during exercise, take your reliever medication again until symptoms have been relieved. It is not recommended that you return to the activity. After exercise, cool down as usual. Asthma symptoms can occur up to half an hour after exercise. Make sure you take your reliever medication if you have symptoms after exercise.

Best and worst exercises for asthma

Swimming is one of the best exercises for asthma because it builds up the muscles you use for breathing. It also exposes the lungs to lots of warm, moist air, which is less likely to trigger asthma symptoms. A comprehensive medical review of eight studies of children and adolescents from 2013 showed that swimming increases lung function and cardiopulmonary fitness, without any serious side effects in patients with stable asthma.

Yoga is another good exercise for asthma. A 2012 study published in the *Journal of Alternative and Complementary Medicine* found that yoga training over 10 weeks significantly improved quality of life scores for women with mild to moderate asthma. Other potential physical activities for people with asthma include:

- walking,
- biking,
- hiking,
- golf, and gymnastics.

No activity has to be off-limits with asthma, but some sports are more likely to trigger asthma symptoms. These include cold-weather sports, like cross-country skiing, and ice hockey, and endurance sports, such as soccer or long-distance running.

****

Appendix 1-Organisations that exist to help and advise those suffering from asthma.

General Support for asthma

Asthma UK www.asthma.org.uk (now known as asthma + lung.uk

The UK's biggest organisation dealing with all aspects of asthma. If you have an enquiry relating to Asthma or Asthma UK including membership, donations, contact the Supporter Care Team, contact the below:

By telephone: 0300 222 5800, Monday to Friday, 9am to 5pm
By email: info@asthma.org.uk
By post: write to:

Supporter Care Team,
Asthma UK,
18 Mansell Street,
London,
E1 8AA.

Please note: The Supporter Care Team are unable to answer any medical queries. If your asthma has been troubling you or you have questions about your medicines or inhalers, please contact the Helpline.

Asthma UK WhatsApp Service

07378 606 728 (9am-5pm, Monday-Friday)

Chat to asthma UK asthma nurse team via WhatsApp. They aim to reply to all your messages within three working days.

British Lung Foundation

0300 222 5800

The British Lung Foundation runs a network of more than 230 'Breathe Easy' support groups for people living with lung conditions.

Asthma Health and Safety at Work

https://hse.gov.uk/asthma

Advice from the Health and Safety Executive about Asthma at Work.

NHS Asthma Advice

https://www.nhs.uk/conditions/asthma

Comprehensive website from the NHS dealing with all aspects of asthma.

Self Management UK

www.selfmanagementuk.org

A charity that runs self-management courses for people with long-term conditions to help them take control of their lives.

Childhood Asthma
NHS England
www.england.nhs.uk/childhood-asthma
A Comprehensive and important website dealing with Childhood Asthma.

Beat Asthma
www.beatasthma.co.uk/resources/young-people-with-asthma/
An organisation with resources tailored to the needs of young people.
On the Beat Asthma site, you will find all the information you need to fully understand your asthma, know how to recognise important symptoms and know how your treatment should be so you can get the best possible control of your asthma. There is also advice for how to look after your asthma in schools and things to help your friends understand more about it too and know what to do if you need their help.

Healthy London and Asthma
www.healthylondon.org/our-work/children-young-people/asthma/
A website dedicated to those with Asthma living in London.

Appendix 2. Useful advice for those suffering from Asthma – Travelling abroad and access to welfare benefits

The below is advice from the NHS for people with Asthma who intend to travel abroad.

Health experts advise preparing for a trip 4 to 6 weeks before travel.

What you'll need when travelling with asthma

Take your usual medicine, along with a copy of your prescriptions and your:

- asthma action plan
- travel insurance documents
- European Health Insurance card for European travel

Things to consider as part of your preparation include:

- an asthma health check
- your asthma triggers
- air travel
- travel vaccinations
- travel insurance
- whether your EHIC is valid in your country of travel after Brexit

Travelling in Europe after Brexit

You will need to check travel requirements with countries concerned now the UK has left the EU. Travel insurance is an absolute necessity.

Asthma health check

See a GP or asthma nurse before you travel to review your personal asthma action plan and make sure it's up to date. If you do not have a personal asthma action plan, now's the time to get one. It'll allow you to recognise deteriorating asthma and alter your treatment to stay well. Find out how you can get medical help, such as a local ambulance or doctor, at your destination. Take spare inhalers in case of loss or theft. You can usually carry them in your hand luggage. Bring enough medicine to last throughout your trip, plus a few extra days. Take a printout of your regular prescriptions, including the names of medicines (brand names and medical names) in case you need medical assistance during your trip or your medicine is lost.

Avoid asthma triggers

If being exposed to feather pillows makes your asthma worse, bring your own non-feather alternative or ask your hotel for a pillow with synthetic filling. If you're sensitive to tobacco smoke, ask your hotel whether you should book a non-smoking room as smoking rules vary from country to country. Some holiday activities, such as scuba diving, may be hazardous to people with asthma and special considerations may apply. Ensure your asthma is fully controlled, as exposure to allergens and viral infections in confined spaces, such as planes and ships, may make your asthma worse.

Air travel with asthma

If you're always short of breath, even when resting, you may need a check-up before you fly because of the reduced oxygen levels at high altitude. Carry all your asthma medicines as hand luggage in case your checked-in luggage goes missing or your medicines are damaged in the baggage hold. Under current security restrictions, you cannot carry containers with liquids, gels or creams that exceed 100ml in your hand luggage.

You can carry essential medicines of more than 100ml on board, but you'll need prior approval from the airline and airport, as well as a letter from your doctor or a prescription. All asthma medicines taken on board should be in their original packaging, with the prescription label and contact details of the pharmacy clearly visible.

For more information, read the British Lung Foundation's advice on air travel with a lung condition.

Travel vaccinations and asthma

A GP or practice nurse can tell you what vaccinations and precautions you need to take for the country you're travelling to. You can have the usual travel jabs that are recommended for your destination unless there are other health reasons for not having them.

Tell a GP or practice nurse if you have recently taken high-dose steroid tablets before you have any vaccinations.

Malaria tablets and asthma

Asthma and its treatment do not usually interfere with malaria tablets.

Travel insurance and asthma

Take out travel insurance and check that it'll cover your asthma. The government always advises UK nationals to take out comprehensive travel insurance when going overseas, both to EU and non-EU destinations. Make sure your insurance has the necessary healthcare cover to ensure you can get any treatment you might need. Talk to a GP and your insurer about how to get the right cover for your asthma and how this affects your travel. Many insurers ask you to get permission from a GP before you travel.

.

Asthma and access to welfare benefits

Prescription charges
If you live in Northern Ireland, Scotland, or Wales, you don't have to pay for prescriptions.

Pre-payment Certificate
In England, many people with asthma qualify for free prescriptions but if you don't and if you have to collect one or more items a month, a Pre-Payment Certificate could save you money.

Low-income scheme
If you are on a low income and don't have many savings, you can apply to the NHS Low Income Scheme which may be able to offer you help with affording your prescriptions.

Help with health costs
If you're struggling financially, you may be able to get help with some health costs.

Travel costs
Help with travel costs to and from hospital is generally possible if you're on a low income or getting certain benefits.

Cold Weather Payment

You may get Cold Weather Payments if you're getting certain benefits. Although this isn't strictly a health-related benefit it's worth knowing if you're eligible. Especially as heating your home properly can prevent damp or temperatures changing room-to-room, which are both things which can trigger asthma.

Winter Fuel Payment

If you were born on or before 5 May 1953, you could get Winter Fuels Payments of between £100 and £300 tax-free to help pay your heating bills. In 2022-2023 there has been an uplift to payments due to the energy crisis and also the cost-of-living crisis. You will have been contacted by your energy company.

You usually get this payment automatically if you get the State Pension or another social security benefit. It's especially important to heat your home well during winter when you have asthma because damp and changing temperatures can trigger asthma symptoms.

Sick pay

If you need time off work because of your asthma, your workplace should have a policy to cover this, or you may be able to get Statutory Sick Pay (also known as SSP). Find out more about working when you have asthma.

Financial support at university

You may worry about affording asthma medicine prescriptions or travel to and from hospitals when you're a student and might not have much money. The good news is there's lots of support available so that you can make sure your asthmas well managed without having to worry about your finances meaning you can get on with enjoying your time at university. Like anyone, you can save money if you need more than one prescription a month by getting a Pre-Payment Certificate. You might also be able to get:

Low Income Scheme - HC1 forms

Some students may be able to get help with NHS costs and prescriptions through the NHS Low Income Scheme. This means you may get a large discount on your prescriptions or you may even get them free, depending on what sources of income you have (including your student loan). You'll need to complete the NHS HC1 claim form. You can order one online on the NHS Business Services Authority website.

Financial problems and help

In England, Wales and Scotland, Turn2Us is a national charity that helps people in financial hardship to gain access to welfare benefits, charitable grants and support services. https://www.turn2us.org.uk. *In addition to the welfare benefits described above, there may be help with a range of other benefits depending on the severity of your asthma. Asthma UK also has comprehensive welfare benefits advice.* In Northern Ireland, Finance Support is a new service that has been created to support people in times of financial need. www.nidirect.gov.uk/articles/extra-financial-support.

****

Sample Asthma Action Plan

My asthma triggers

Taking my asthma medicine each day will help reduce my reaction to these triggers. Avoid them where possible will also help.

> People with allergies need to be extra careful as attacks can be more severe

My asthma review

I should have at least one routine asthma review every year **I will bring:**

- My action plan to see if it needs updating
- Any inhalers and spacers I have, to check I'm using them correctly and in the best way.
- Any questions about my asthma and how to cope with it

Next asthma review date:-----------------

GP/ asthma nurse contact

Name
Phone number

Out-of-hours contact number
(ask your GP surgery who to call when they are closed)

Name
Phone number

How to use it

Your written asthma action plan can help you stay on top of your asthma... To get the most from it, you could..

1. **Put it somewhere easy for you and your family to find-** like your fridge door, noticeboard, or bedside table
2. **Keep a photo of it on your mobile, phone or tablet-** so you can check it whenever you are. You can also send it to a family member or friend, so they know what to do if your asthma symptoms get worse.
3. **Check in with it regularly-** put a note on your calendar, or a monthly reminder on your phone to read it through. Are you remembering to use your day-to-day asthma medicine? Do you know what to do if your symptoms get worse?

4. **Take it to every healthcare appointment about your asthma-**including A&E/ consultant. Ask your GP or asthma nurse to update it if their advice for you changes.

Every day asthma care:

My asthma is being managed well:
- with this daily routine I should expect/ aim to have no symptoms
- If I've not had any symptoms or needed my reliever inhaler for at least 12 weeks, I can ask my GP or asthma nurse to review my medicines in case they can reduce the dose
- My personal best peak flow is

My daily asthma routine:

My preventer inhaler (insert name/colour)

I need to take my preventer inhaler every day even when I feel well

I take   puff(s) in the morning
and   puff(s) at night

My reliever inhaler (insert name/colour)

I take my **reliever** inhaler only if I need to
I take   puff(s) of my reliever if any of these things happen:

- I"m wheezing
- My chest feels tight
- I'm finding it hard to breath
- I'm coughing

Other medicines and advices (eg spacers) I use for my asthma every day:

When I feel worse:

My asthma is getting worse if I'm experiencing any of these:
- My symptoms are coming back (wheezing, tightness in my chest, feeling breathless, (cough).
- I am waking up at night.
- My symptoms are interfering with my usual day-to-day activities (eg at work, exercising)
- I am using my reliever inhaler three times a week or more
- My peak flow drops to below   ....

URGENT! If you need your reliever inhaler more than every four hours, you're having an asthma attack and you need to take emergency action now.

What I can do to get on top of my asthma now:

If I haven't been using my preventer inhaler, I'll start using it regularly again or if I have been using it

Increase my preventer inhaler dose to.....puffs ....times a day until my symptoms have gone and my peak flow is back to my personal best

Take my reliever inhaler as needed (up to ....puffs every four hours)

I carry my reliever inhaler with me when I'm out.

URGENT! See a doctor or nurse within 24 hours if you get worse at any time or you haven't improved after seven days.

In an asthma attack

I'm having an asthma attack if I'm experiencing any of these
• My reliever inhaler is not helping or I need it more than every four hours. • I find it difficult to walk and talk • I find it difficult to breath. • I'm wheezing a lot or have a very tight chest or I'm coughing a lot • My peak flow is below ....

What to do in an asthma attack

1. Sit up straight – try to keep calm

2. Take one puff of your reliever inhaler (usually blue) every 30 –60 seconds, up to a maximum of 10 puffs

3. If you feel worse at any point OR you don'y feel better after 10 puffs call 999 for an ambulance

4. Repeat step2 after 15 minutes while you're waiting for an ambulance

After an asthma attack
See your GP within 48 hours to make sure you're not at risk of another attack. If you get worse see them urgently. Finish any medicines they prescribe you., even if you start to feel better. If you don't improve after treatment, see your GP urgently.

INDEX

Emerald Guides
www.straightforwardbooks.co.uk

Titles in the Emerald Series:

Law

Guide to Bankruptcy

Conducting Your Own Court case

Guide to Consumer law

Creating a Will

Guide to Family Law

Guide to Employment Law

Guide to European Union Law

Guide to Health and Safety Law

Guide to Criminal Law

Guide to Landlord and Tenant Law

Guide to the English Legal System

Guide to Housing Law

Guide to Marriage and Divorce

Guide to The Civil Partnerships Act

Guide to The Law of Contract

The Path to Justice

You and Your Legal Rights

Powers of Attorney

Managing Separation and Divorce

Health

Guide to Combating Child Obesity

Asthma Begins at Home

Alternative Health and Alternative Remedies

Explaining Arthritis

Explaining Parkinsons

Finding Asperger Syndrome in the Family-A Book of Answers

Explaining Autism Spectrum Disorder

Explaining Bi-Polar Disorder

The Complete Guide to the Digestive System

Music

How to Survive and Succeed in the Music Industry

General

A Practical Guide to Obtaining probate

A Practical Guide to Residential Conveyancing

Writing The Perfect CV

Keeping Books and Accounts-A Small Business Guide

Business Start Up-A Guide for New Business

Writing True Crime

Becoming a Professional Writer

Writing your Autobiography

For details of the above titles published in the Emerald Guides Series go to: www.straightforwardbooks.co.uk

Further books in the Emerald 'Explaining' Series

EXPLAINING ARTHRITIS
LIVING WITH AND CONTROLLING ARTHRITIS
REVISED EDITION 2023
ELLEN BAXENDALE
25th March 2023 978-1-80236-169-8
£9.99

EXPLAINING AUTISM
Second Edition
CLARE LAWRENCE
SEPT 2017   978-1-84716-726-2
£9.99

EXPLAINING PARKINSON'S
REVISED EDITION 2023
DOREEN JARRETT
25th March 2023   978-1-80236-171-1
£9.99

EXPLAINING DIABETES
REVISED EDITION
DOREEN JARRETT
25 August 2022   978-1-80236-092-9
£9.99

EXPLAINING BI-POLAR DISORDER

A Comprehensive Guide to the Symptoms and Manifestation of
Bi-Polar Disorder

SECOND EDITION
DOREEN JARRETT
25 June 2019   978-1-84716-944-0
£9.99